Fighting for Survival

The Anangu of Uluru and Kata Tjuta

Liz Thompson

Heinemann
LIBRARY

A royalty goes to the Anangu

First published 1998 by
Heinemann Library
an imprint of Reed Educational & Professional Publishing,
18–22 Salmon Street, Port Melbourne, Victoria 3207, Australia
(a division of Reed International Books Pty Ltd, ACN 001-002-357).

ℛ A Reed Elsevier company

© Text and photographs Liz Thompson 1998
Copyright of artwork and quotations remains with the individual
artists.
pages 32–33, The artist, Maraku Arts
page 36, The artist, Maraku Arts
page 41, Barbara Tjikatu and Rene Kulijta
page 42, Barbara Tjikatu
page 45, Jennifer Taylor

02 01 00 99 98
10 9 8 7 6 5 4 3 2 1

Edited by Jane Pearson
Original design by Jo Waite Design
Paged by Serendipity Studio
Typeset in Optima 11/14pt
Production by Cindy Smith
Film separations by Type Scan, Adelaide
Printed in Hong Kong by H&Y Printing Ltd

Cover photograph: Nellie Patterson in front of her house at
Mutitjulu.
Photograph page 1: Alkwari
Photograph on pages 16, 25 top, 27 bottom by Stanley Breedan.
Photograph on pages 13, 44 by David Curl.

The information on pages 34–35 is drawn from the Uluru–Kata Tjuta
Cultural Centre and notes from the Maraku Arts & Crafts Centre.
World Heritage information on page 15 comes from *World Heritage
– Australia's World Heritage*, Department of the Environment, Sport
and Territories.

*National Library of Australia
Cataloguing-in-publication data:*

Thompson, Liz, 1963– .
The Anangu of Uluru-Kata Tjuta.

  Bibliography.
  Includes index.

  ISBN 1 86391 907 4.

  1. Anangu (Australian people) – Social life and customs –
Juvenile literature. 2. Anangu (Australian people) –
Foreign influences – Juvenile literature. I. Title.
(Series : Fighting for survival).

306.0899915

Acknowledgements

Thanks to the Governing Committee of the
Mutitjulu Community Inc for permission to
publish this book.

Thanks to many people for assistance in the
creation of this book: Peter Wilson and
Karina Lester for their work as translators.
Special thanks to Barbara Tjikatu and
Mantajarra Wilson for their help and
guidance.

Thanks also to Paul Josif, co-ordinator,
Office for Joint Management, and to Parks
Australia North staff and the Board of
Management for permission to work within
the park and with the Mutitjulu community.

Contents

Judy Kunmanara

Introduction

A nomadic people

Amongst the indigenous people of Australia, different Aboriginal groups were responsible for looking after particular areas of the country. The A̲nangu, Yankuntjatjara and Pitjantjatjara speaking peoples, are from the Western Desert area of Australia and are responsible for a large area of land which includes what is now Ulu̲ru–Kata Tju̲ta National Park. There is evidence they have lived in this area for over 22 000 years. A̲nangu make up a large part of the Mu̲titjulu community, which lies one kilometre from the base of Ulu̲ru.

A̲nangu traditionally led a subsistence existence based on hunting and gathering. They walked many kilometres each day looking for food and water. A̲nangu found all they needed on the land. For shelter they built spinifex windbreaks, called *yuu*, and they slept naked around fires. They traded in ceremonial objects like the pearl shells which came from the north coast and resources such as stone. For thousands of years they lived like this, until the arrival of the first Europeans in the 1800s.

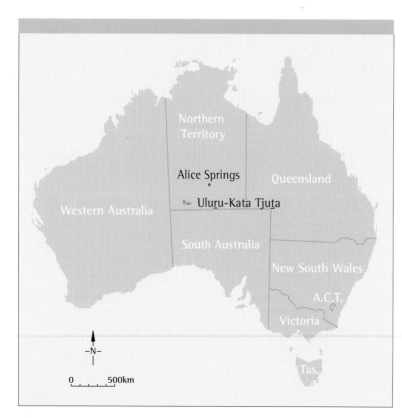

Terra nullius

When Europeans arrived in Australia they took control of the land. Ignoring the rights of ownership of indigenous inhabitants, they justified their claims to the land by declaring that Australia was 'terra nullius' – a land devoid of humans and therefore belonging to no one. This idea was based on the notion that unless land was being cultivated or farmed it was not owned. A̲nangu led a nomadic life, neither farming nor cultivating the land. A country without a ruler recognised by European authorities was also thought to be free for the taking. The Europeans' justification for taking the land is now acknowledged by the Australian High Court to be seriously flawed.

Uluru

Europeans at Uluru

Just over one hundred years ago, Ernest Giles and William Gosse became the first Europeans to see Uluru and Kata Tjuta, and they named them Ayers Rock and Mount Olga. Until the 1930s, the arrival of Europeans had not had too serious an impact on traditional Anangu life. This contact intensified however as missionaries, native welfare patrol officers, prospectors, dingo scalp hunters and pastoralists moved further into the centre of Australia. Airstrips were constructed near Uluru in 1930 and 1933 which meant people could get to the remote area more easily.

The depletion of foods

When pastoralism began, cattle ate many of the plants that formed a vital part of the Anangu diet. Small mammals also suffered from the loss of these plants and the disturbance of their habitats, and became more scarce. They were also hunted and eaten by feral cats and foxes. These mammals had been an important source of food for Anangu. Water sources were also affected as many rock holes were polluted by wandering stock. These problems were aggravated by a long drought in the 1930s.

These and the many other hardships experienced by Anangu brought them into conflict with the authorities. From hunger and frustration Aboriginal people hunted the pastoralists' cattle. Reports in the Cultural Centre at Uluru–Kata Tjuta tell of people being led away in neck irons and leg chains. Policies at the time did very little to protect the Aboriginal people. By the 1940s the patterns of land use which had allowed Anangu to live off their land had, to a large extent, been broken down by the pastoral industry.

The stolen generation

Stolen Generation

From the 1930s to the 1960s the Australian government's policy was one of assimilation. This meant that the government's aim was to absorb Aboriginal people into European society. It is from this misguided policy that the generation now known as the 'stolen children' came to be. Any children who were born of mixed descent, or who looked vaguely 'white', were removed from their homelands and their parents, and institutionalised or fostered out to white families. The official view was that these children would grow up in the European world and so learn the European ways, and slowly Aboriginal culture would die out. Some people behind the policy also believed Aboriginal children removed from their natural families and raised by Europeans would have greater opportunities as they grew up. What in fact resulted was a generation of children, and parents, who continue to suffer from the emotional trauma of being separated. Many of these children now talk of experiencing confusion in relation to their identity after being denied access to their own families and culture for so long.

I got it easier today 'cause we got our land back. They don't take any children away that are half caste like me now. Back then I would have lost everything. My brother got taken away but I was around when they didn't do those things anymore. Everything's changed since European people came. I'm half European. It's not easy, people give you a hard time, course they do, they'll always do it.
Peter Wilson

Peter Wilson

Today almost all young children at Mutitjulu grow up with their parents and attend local schools in or close to the community.

My mother was taken away like all the others from the lost generation. The police in those days they just went around and collected them. Her mother and grandmothers used to paint her up with ashes and stuff, so that she would pass off as a full blood and so that she couldn't be taken away, wouldn't be caught. When light skin kids were caught they were just taken, no questions asked and they were told their parents were dead, my mum always thought her mother was dead after she was taken away. They weren't allowed to speak their language no more, they would get a hiding for that, not allowed to talk any Aboriginal.

Connie Calma; her mother was taken away. Connie was born in Darwin and only returned to her mother's country at Uluru when she was in her forties.

Settlement

From the 1930s onwards there was a lot of movement as A̲nangu began to move away from their life on the land and settled in certain areas. People tell of making camps around cattle stations or missions. From these settlements they were often hired for work, particularly for help in stockwork and building roads. For their labour, they received rations of flour, sugar and tea or blankets. At the time, the government was making an effort to reduce the dingo population and offered rewards for dingo scalps. White people known as 'doggers' often bought dingo scalps from the Aboriginal people, exchanging the scalps for flour, blankets or other material goods.

House warm one, we can't go live in bush, we might get cold. When we were in bush we made big camp, windbreak, big fire. We went hunting, digging for witchetty grub, *maku*, make warm and walking make warm too, travelling, walking. We like good house, we don't like no good one, we like clothes and blanket, make warm, new way, old way, two way. Old way we sit down, no blanket.

Barbara Tjikatu

Outside Barbara Tjikatu's house

People still go hunting, but today Anangu buy most of their food from the store at Mutitjulu.

We grown up in that mission school at Ernabella. We were living naked before, no clothes, long time. Some little girls, little boys and big ones too, naked one, sitting down. Long time ago everyone naked. 1973 or 1974 finish, start wearing clothes. A whitefella minister came along, said, come don't put naked one all the time. When Winter comes gotta make it warm with jumper and all that. Cause some get flu, get sick and pass away. When I was naked one, little girl, we sit down everywhere, no tent, no blanket, my mother make spinifex *wurli* and fire and make really warm one. But with minister at Ernabella got that tent and blanket and everything but no clothes and then I was walking naked one day to school only with blanket and they take blanket, whitefella school teacher and throw it in the cupboard and say you gotta sit down naked. They hose us with cold water all over, us naked ones, no clothes. After school we grab that blanket, they give it back.

Nellie Patterson

From the work now we've learned to live in a house. This new way we're living now, this is the way things are in the western world. Long ago we had to go off and get wood and make fire. Gotta build it up in night that fire, restless sleep. We had to build windbreak, get right in. We'd stay a while, about three days and then we move and make another shelter like that. When wind changes have to move it round. This one easier (referring to his house), got walls and pot belly stove. It's nice and warm here.

Tony Tjamiwa

Aboriginal land rights

Ever since the arrival of Europeans, Aboriginal rights to, or ownership of, land had not been recognised at all. The Aboriginal Land Rights (Northern Territory) Act, passed in 1976, represented the beginnings of a move away from the legal concept of 'terra nullius' which had been used to justify the complete dispossession of the indigenous inhabitants of Australia. The Act gave perpetual freehold title of Northern Territory Aboriginal reserves to the Aboriginal Traditional Owners. At the same time, it began the slow process of recognising traditional ownership in certain areas of the Northern Territory through a land claims process.

Reserves

During the 1920s a large area which included Uluṟu–Kata Tjuṯa had been established as an Aboriginal Reserve. In reality, the reserves had done little to protect the Aboriginal communities from the influences that arrived during the 1930s. In 1958, as a result of the combined pressure from gold prospectors who wanted to explore the area and a campaign to gain access to the Uluṟu–Kata Tjuṯa region for the purposes of tourism, Uluṟu–Kata Tjuṯa was removed from the Aboriginal reserve and became a 'tourist and wildlife reserve'.

Tony Tjamiwa is one of the senior custodians of Tjukurpa at Uluṟu.

Frustrations

Until the 1970s, the Traditional Owners of Uluṟu–Kata Tjuṯa were not consulted in the management or running of the area as a tourist and wildlife reserve. This was a cause for increasing concern to them. Larger numbers of tourists were arriving and Anangu were worried the country was not being looked after properly. Visitors had no understanding of sacred sites and what they meant to Anangu. They frequently walked through sacred areas, took photographs of inappropriate places and invaded the privacy of Anangu who lived around the base of Uluru. In addition there was inadequate environmental management. For example, Anangu were no longer permitted to practise traditional 'patch burning', a method they had used to control the sweep of wild fires. As a result, a fire which swept through the park in the 1970s wiped out nearly 75 per cent of the vegetation and was responsible for the deaths of many animals.

At a meeting in 1973, traditional Aboriginal landowners expressed their dissatisfaction at a meeting with the Federal House of Representatives Standing Committee on Environment and Conservation. After listening to the issues raised by Anangu it was decided several steps would be taken, these included the establishment of an Aboriginal camp, the protection of important sacred sites through the erection of fences, the establishment of an Advisory Committee with Aboriginal members and the employment of Aboriginal rangers.

These things did little to relieve the overall frustration felt by Traditional Owners that the land was not in their hands to be taken care of in the way they felt it should be. This feeling was aggravated by restrictions on hunting and collecting firewood in the park which went against traditional practices of hunting and gathering. By the early 1980s Uluru–Kata Tjuta had become a major source of revenue for the Northern Territory because of the huge numbers of tourists it attracted. As a result of the perceived loss of tourist revenue and the political opposition to Aboriginal land rights, the Northern Territory government fought the handback to the Traditional Owners.

Mutitjulu waterhole, one of the sacred areas at Uluru. It is now protected by appropriate park management strategies. The Mutitjulu community was named after this waterhole.

Land claims

I've been talking about this place for a very long time and at last my whole spirit is relieved that finally we've got Ayers Rock back. Uluru and Kata Tjuta are safe at last. The elder women and the elder men are completely happy. Everything is happy because we Anangu have been given our Aboriginal land. We've been given back our Aboriginal spirit.

Nellie Patterson, in Tjukurpa Waakaripai – Working Together, ANCA, 1995

As a result of the Aboriginal Land Rights Act it became possible for Aboriginal Traditional Owners to claim unalienated crown land for which they had strong traditional connections. Unalienated land is crown land, over which no one holds freehold title, a mining, pastoral or commercial lease.

The Uluru–Kata Tjuta national park has now been returned to its Traditional Owners.

It also includes land that has been set aside for public use. A claim was made by the Traditional Owners for the Uluru–Kata Tjuta area but was heavily opposed. Those individuals and organisations who often fought against land claims were the Northern Territory Government, as well as mining companies and pastoralists who believed Aboriginal ownership of certain areas of land would make the business of mining or running stock more difficult for them. It was decided Uluru–Kata Tjuta was alienated crown land because it was leased to the Director of Australian Parks and Wildlife.

It wasn't until 11 November 1983 that Aboriginal title to Uluru was acknowledged. It was officially handed back on 26 October 1985 in a ceremony at the base of Uluru. One of the conditions of handback was that the Anangu would lease the park back to the Director of Australian National Parks and Wildlife Service (ANPWS). These leaseback arrangements have become known as 'working together' or joint management.

That's my place out there. The whitefella knows no stories out there. That's my place I own. My father was born there and I was born there. Whitefellas haven't got their stories or dreamings out there – I don't try and take away Melbourne or Adelaide… we want the white men to come and visit our place, not take it away. They must know it belongs to us. Now I am left with just my tent and broken promises.

Nipper Winmati (Dec), one of the Traditional Owners of Uluṟu–Kata Tjuṯa, speaking to reporters outside the hall where the Commissioner had announced his finding that the park was alienated land

Two days after the finding, the Traditional Owners produced a petition they wished to present to the Prime Minister. Part of that petition read:

We cannot accept however, that someone else in Canberra can hold the papers to our land. It is not his country – it is ours. White people should show their recognition of our rights and give us the freehold title. We will make an agreement to lease the land to the National Parks Service if we can have a say about what is done. We must protect our law, our sacred places from visitors. These are for Aboriginals alone and essential to us if our culture is to survive.

Uluṟu – An Aboriginal History of Ayers Rock

Being born into that place, touching the earth, naked, that's the way Aṉangu inherit land, by being born into a place.

Barbara Tjikatu, in Uluṟu – An Aboriginal history of Ayers Rock

'This,' said the new Prime Minister, Bob Hawke, 'is an historic decision and is a measure of the willingness of this Government, on behalf of the Australian people, to recognise the just and legitimate claims of a people who have been dispossessed of their land, but who have never lost their spiritual attachment to that land.'

Uluṟu – An Aboriginal history of Ayers Rock

The handback ceremony,
26 October 1985

Joint management

Board of management

Management of Uluṟu–Kata Tjuṯa is based on the philosophy of 'working together'. The lease agreement at the time of the handback ensured that Anangu people would jointly manage the park and be involved in all decisions relating to it. The agreement set out that Anangu would hold the majority on the Board of Management which makes all the big decisions. The Office for Joint Management ensures the community's wishes and the Traditional Owners' wishes are represented. The Board has 10 members – six

Rupert Goodwin, one of the Anangu rangers at Uluṟu–Kata Tjuṯa National Park

A thorny devil and grasshopper, two of the many animals found in the Uluṟu–Kata Tjuṯa National Park

of these are Aṉangu. The rest of the Board is made up of the Director of Parks Australia, one person nominated by the Federal Minister responsible for the environment and one nominated by the Federal Minister responsible for tourism, and a scientist specialising in arid lands ecology. The Board is involved in issues affecting the park. It discusses what work should be done, if more walking tracks should be developed, where roads should go, the protection of sacred sites, the staff who will work in the park, what they will do, and how they will be trained. The Board makes major policy decisions; it listens to park managers, it approves the consultants who do specialist work, it discusses money and budgets, as well as a multitude of other things to do with the management of the park, as prescribed in the lease and the plan of management.

World Heritage

Uluṟu-Kata Tjuṯa National Park received World Heritage Listing for its natural values in 1987 and values as a cultural landscape in 1994. What this means is that its exceptional natural beauty and geological qualities are seen to hold value for the whole world. This area has been listed culturally because it is 'an outstanding example of traditional human land-use', and 'directly associated with living traditions and beliefs'. World Heritage Listing is not only an acknowledgement, the Commonwealth Government also has an international obligation to protect and conserve World Heritage Property.

Diary

Thursday 17th June

I arrived here yesterday to attend a Muṯitjulu Community Council Meeting. I had sent a letter talking about the series *Fighting for Survival* and requesting permission to work on a book with the Aṉangu. Like all such requests, it must go before the Board and, depending on the request, also to the Muṯitjulu Community Council for approval. Several Aṉangu Board members were present. I showed them one of the books from the series and talked about why I felt it was a good thing to do. I explained that it would teach people all over Australia about the Aṉangu way. The Aṉangu said Aboriginal communities all over Australia were teaching their children culture, why did they need a book. I said that children living in Aboriginal communities had the opportunity to learn but thousands of others didn't. One of the women, Mantajarra Wilson, started to say to the group that this book was an opportunity to teach people all over Australia about the Aṉangu way – tell them about bush tucker and Tjukurpa culture. Tony Tjamiwa, another Aṉangu board member, agreed with her. Then the non-Aṉangu liaison officer, another non-Aṉangu woman and I were asked to leave the room whilst the Council talked about the proposal. Shortly afterwards they called us back and said they thought the book was a good idea. Permission for me to work with the Aṉangu on the book was granted.

Working together

Joint management

Joint management of the park, based on the idea of 'working together', has led to a marriage of Anangu and non-Anangu knowledge in many areas. Several Anangu rangers have been employed and traditional Anangu practices have been included in the park management.

Traditional burning

In the past, Anangu often carried fire sticks as they walked across the country setting alight small patches of land. This was a form of traditional land management. Not only did it prevent large scale fires from sweeping across the landscape, destroying thousands of plants and animals, it provided new growth of soft grasses and small shrubs. Both these were a wonderful food source for many animals. The method of what is called 'patch-burning' meant the fresh new plants that grew on burnt ground were always close to well-established old plants which provided animals with shelter. The traditional burning practices of Anangu are based on thousands of years of experience. Since the park was handed back to the Traditional Owners, patch burning has become a recognised part of managing the area for the protection of wildlife and their habitats.

Julian Barry, when he was the park's training officer, with four trainee rangers: Nyinku Jingo, Andy Panpanpalala, Rupert Goodwin and Akana Campbell.

The story of the *lungkata*, or blue-tongued lizard, tells of how he moved through the area patch burning as he came from Kata Tjuta. That's part of the law. Law is the basis of patch burning.
Rupert Goodwin

Senior Anangu men and Anangu rangers work alongside non-Anangu park staff showing them how to burn certain areas at particular times of the year. Now fires are often started with drip torches rather than smouldering sticks. Instead of walking for miles, people travel in 4-wheel drives looking for the right places to burn. Despite the different techniques, Anangu still use the same knowledge and understanding of the landscape and climate when choosing areas to be burnt.

Fauna survey

The fauna survey which took place at Uluṟu–Kata Tjuṯa was the first of its kind in Australia. It combined traditional Aṉangu knowledge of animals with scientific knowledge. During the research, scientists marked out areas and set up traps in which animals were counted and weighed. Aṉangu shared their knowledge of animal behaviour, gained as a result of living on the land for thousands of years. Aṉangu are highly skilled in reading animal tracks and were able to lead scientists to many animals they otherwise wouldn't have found. This combination of knowledge helped to create the most thorough fauna survey ever produced in Australia. As a result, management practices designed to protect vulnerable and endangered species are being put in place.

> Part of joint management is teaching rangers land management in traditional way – Tjukurpa, our ancestral stories, keeping that Tjukurpa, those cultural stories alive. This is law from our grandfathers and grandmothers, passed down. Nothing has changed.
> **Tony Tjamiwa**

> I was standing and looking and learning. We came around the park and at night we check at the viewing spots late because if there's a car there, might be someone got lost on the rock, then we radio the ranger and they come and help. We check the whole park, no car sitting, we know they've all gone to Yulara. If there's no one left in the park we get on the radio and say the park is closed and they say, 'OK see you in the morning'. That's the way they teach me. I'm a ranger now and I know everything. Many tourists come from all over the world, they come and listen to me when we take them on Mala walk and I today I'm a smart man.
> **Rupert Goodwin**

> I'm really happy us today coming together. It's good we are coming together to support that work of the park. We're always learning about this, always teaching it. We've got to come together to look after the park properly and do that work.
> **Barbara Tjikadu**

Tjukurpa

Life for all Anangu people is governed by what is known as Tjukurpa. Tjukurpa is a body of knowledge which has often been mistakenly called 'the Dreaming' by non-Aboriginals. Tjukurpa contains Aboriginal law and religious beliefs. It outlines social codes of behaviour, and teaches about medicine, hunting and childbirth. Every aspect of life is touched on in the Tjukurpa and it is this body of knowledge which defines the way Anangu live.

Tjukurpa tells of how the physical aspects of the earth were brought into existence through the journeys of a number of ancestral beings. Anangu believe that in the beginning the world was flat and featureless. As the ancestral creatures journeyed across the country certain events took place. During these events, the physical features of the earth and all living species were created. Every rock, every waterhole, cave, river or mountain relates to a particular event that took place during these journeys. Anangu are the descendants of these beings and are now responsible for looking after and caring for the country their ancestors created.

Within the Tjukurpa there are different levels of knowledge. Some stories are more secret and sacred than others. The possession of secret knowledge brings with it a great responsibility to take care of it and pass it on to the right people.

The Tjukurpa stories tell of Tjati, a small red lizard who travelled to Uluru during the creation. Tjati threw his kali, throwing stick, towards Uluru and it landed here in the north face. As Tjati scooped his hands into the rock, trying to retrieve his kali, he created these hollows at the place called Walaritja.

Learning Tjukurpa

Uluru and Kata Tjuta and all the surrounding landscape has its own Tjukurpa stories that tell of how these particular rock formations came into existence. Some of the major stories in this area are the *Mala* (Rufous hare wallaby) Tjukurpa, the *Liru* (poisonous snake) Tjukurpa, the *Kuniya* (woma python) Tjukurpa and the *Lungkata* (blue-tongued lizard) Tjukurpa. As older relatives walked with the children across the country looking for food and water they pointed out aspects of the country and related the stories to them. They also taught Tjukurpa using dance, ceremony and song. In this way the landscape became like a book that children were able to read as the elders taught them how to interpret it. All Tjukurpa stories have many levels, some are public and able to be heard by all people, some are secret and sacred – only known by certain people, usually initiated elders. It is the public interpretation of the stories which is taught to small children. As they grow and become men and women, they are taught deeper, more secret levels of the same stories. Today the Tjukurpa is still the body of law which forms the basis of Anangu life.

Young men went to missions, they learnt and we can't let go, can't leave it alone and what we know from those missionary days we want to pass on the good things, but also want to pass on Tjukurpa. Because both bible and Tjukurpa as we get older teaches us about life, spirit. God's given us life, so we must give thanks. We still got that law, still got our Tjukurpa, still got the law of our grandmothers and grandfathers. We still go and do ceremony all the time. During the week we follow our stories, our Tjukurpa. On Sunday we go to church.
Tony Tjamiwa

Judy Kunmanara

Traditional education

Traditionally young Anangu children learnt by example. Girls learnt to collect bush tucker, prepare food and medicine. They walked with their mothers and grandmothers for many miles each day gathering fruits and seeds and collecting water. They learnt how to make wooden bowls and digging sticks. Boys learnt how to hunt and follow animal tracks. They were shown how to make spears, spearthrowers, boomerangs, and how to cook kangaroo. Children continue to learn by watching their older relatives.

Children learnt the Tjukurpa stories from older Anangu who pointed things out to them as they travelled over the land. One of the stories tells how these holes and dark marks were created on the surface of the rock. Long ago, the kuniya (pythons) arrived at Uluru. One of the kuniya women was carrying her eggs and she buried these. However the liru (poisonous snake) warriors approached and attacked the kuniya. These hole marks on the south-west face are the marks of the liru warriors' spears and the dark stains are their transformed bodies.

Initiation

Both boys and girls go through certain ceremonies during their teenage years. There is a very clear division made between boys and men, and the time during which a child becomes a man is marked by ceremonies. To this day what happens at these ceremonies remains sacred knowledge shared only by initiated men. Traditionally, if any man revealed the secrets of initiation or, for that matter, information about men's sacred sites, it was not uncommon for him to be killed by other members of the group. Once a man has been initiated, he no longer mixes and plays with young girls as he did whilst a boy. He is now considered to be a man and spends his time in the company of men. Today initiation ceremonies continue to take place amongst the Anangu and these customs are still observed.

Sometime we teach the children, learning to throw little spear. We throw paddy melon and they got little spear and they throw it at the melon. Father or big brother teaching them for kangaroo. When they hit kangaroo they really smart, they hunting man. Same as little girl teaching for hunting honey-ant or witchetty-grub or fruits or water. One bowl for bush tucker, one for water, that way. In the bush they teaching young boys and girls like this.
Rupert Goodwin

Traditional teaching is important, oh yeah, it really is. Ours comes first, our school comes first and European school is not that far behind. Without that traditional teaching who are you. Same with all cultures if you don't do that, then you're no one.
Peter Wilson

We collectively have learnt about law at Uluru as small children. We learnt about the country as we grew up, walking around we looked at springs, soakages, no bores then, flowing waters and rockholes. We travelled, seeing things in the country and learning about the place of things in that way. We learnt about running country, putting up fire signal to tell people where we are and what we're doing.
Barbara Tjikadu, from Uluru–Kata Tjuta Cultural Centre

I don't read and write. I hold that law within myself and I teach that way. Kids go to school today and learning that way but we still take kids out bush and teach them about Tjukurpa.
Barbara Tjikatu

Cave paintings were used as a method of teaching Tjukurpa. Elders used certain symbols and images to describe Tjukurpa stories. They painted with natural ochres and earth pigments found in the local environment. Pictures were layered one on top of another each time the area was used. There are several such 'teaching' sites around the base of Uluru.

It's important to have that very close family structure. Mum and Dad will always be the guardians of all those in the family but Mum will always be really close to the daughter and the father will always be close to the son. It's important to listen to these senior people. Your grandmothers are really important. In old times when Mum is off gathering and doing all the work during the day then the young girls' time would be spent with their grandmothers, all the time, listening to the stories. This is who you are connected to. This is how you survive and so on, passing on all that knowledge. So family is very important. You need one another – they are very important to you.
Karina Lester

Schools

All the young children at Mutitjulu go to school together. Sometimes there are as many as 40 children, usually between the ages of about four and 14, in the same class. Manolis, the teacher, gets around the difference by teaching everyone the same subject but varying the approach for each age level. If he's teaching maths, the older children might be using measurements and working out heights and widths of objects while smaller children play with building blocks and learn to count, add and subtract.

The school uses its own resources rather than spending a lot of money buying new books. Many of the interesting activities at the school are recorded by Manolis with a digital camera. He transfers these images to a computer and makes picture books that include photographs of the children and their own stories. Manolis plans to show the children how to use the camera and computer so they can start making their own books.

Traditional teaching

On Mondays children go out with a number of Anangu parents and sometimes a ranger. During the day children are shown how to look for traditional bush tucker and check for animal tracks. Sometimes the elders will teach stories from the Tjukurpa as the group travel through the landscape.

Diary

Monday 23rd June

The school room at Mutitjulu is filled with brightly coloured drawings and mobiles which hang from the ceiling. In one room a small store is set up from which kids sell empty bottles of water and packets of soap, learning how to add and subtract as they charge and pay for the goods. Manolis, the teacher, tells me the children love school and I can believe it as I watch them rush in through the door and begin to draw on large pieces of paper. Other smaller children put on coloured plastic helmets and pick up plastic saws and hammers to begin work as carpenters in the playground. A couple of young boys sit at the computer and Tina and Verne begin to read. When it is time to leave, Manolis has to encourage the kids more than three times to pack up and get ready to go home.

Children are also taught traditional skills at school which includes classes with elders learning traditional stories. Here a child paints a Tjukurpa story with acrylics on a board.

Children at Mutitjulu with painted animal masks they made in school. The teacher then took photographs of them with their masks and these were used in one of the school booklets he produced.

Cross-cultural learning

The children from Mutitjulu often visit the school at the Yulara resort and children from the school at Yulara visit Mutitjulu school. The Anangu children have taken the non-Aboriginal Yulara students to visit the Maraku Arts Centre where they have learnt many things including how the wood for Aboriginal carvings is collected and how artefacts are carved, rubbed and polished with vegetable oil. They visit the cultural centre and go out on bush tucker excursions to find honey-ants or bush-tomatoes. The Mutitjulu children teach the Yulara school children what to look for, how to note that if particular moths are under a tree that is the place to dig for witchetty grubs. Through this process the non-Aboriginal children are learning about the Anangu and how they live.

Secondary school

Until very recently if children wanted to go on to secondary or tertiary education they had to travel about 450 kilometres to Alice Springs and live far away from their families. Now a new high school has opened near Yulara. Even though the children still sleep over at the school, it is only 20 minutes away from the community. Students attend the school on a rotational basis. For four weeks young men attend, whilst girls learn at a school-room at Mutitjulu. At the end of the four weeks, the young men return to go to school at Mutitjulu and the girls attend the new high school. This takes the traditional Anangu customs into account – once boys have undergone initiation, it is not considered appropriate for them to attend school with girls.

Like long time ago my grandma teaching own way, culture way, and that's why I'm teaching my grandchild. Make it strong, look after traditional culture, really strong way. Some other people losing culture, lot of people losing culture, but we know, from when I'm learning from grandma and I'm teaching my children, make 'em straight true for traditional way. Children go to school and learning for whitefella way and after that go back to traditional way. Two way learning. Whitefella school important because all the little one can't listen English properly, they need learning English for two way, for learning for work, for money line, when they grow up, so they can get a job. There's two way, traditional way and money line.

Nellie Patterson

Bush tucker

Gathering

Traditionally the collecting of bush tucker by Anangu took up a considerable amount of time. Men, women and children would constantly be looking at the landscape as they walked, searching not only for signs of animals to hunt but also for the myriad of fruits, berries and seeds that provided much of their diet. It was usually women and young girls who gathered these foods using their bowls and digging sticks. Bush foods were prepared in a variety of different ways: many berries were made into a pulp and mixed with water into a kind of soup, seeds were ground, mixed with water into a paste and often baked in the fire embers and used for medicine.

Tiku, one of the Anangu women who work with Anangu Tours, showing some of the many seeds and berries that make up part of traditional Anangu diet.

Although women and young girls continue to gather bush tucker and prepare it for themselves and their families, there are many other kinds of foods that Anangu now eat. With the arrival of the store and packaged food, Anangu are less-reliant on bush tucker. Because buying food from the store doesn't involve walking for hours and hours each day, people find it is an easier way to feed their families. But the food is not nearly as nutritious, and people need money to buy food from the store.

When they lived in bush might be walking 50 miles (80 kilometres) to find water. That's hard time and water might be in the ground and they're digging for water. Then they had only water, no tea and sugar, only light people, fit. Now just like white people, got house, got car, driving everywhere, no walking, no fit, go to supermarket, buy all sweet things in body, biscuit, cake, sweet, coke, diet-coke and no walking all driving. Can only go halfway 'cause we got short-wind. Not like olden day now, today not living in bush, we are new people living in a house and I always think early days they were good thing. Now not walking far and always go to doctor. Today I always go to doctor and taking many tablet, got many tablet in my home and that's why I'm sad. I'm thinking old days are better. Walking to Ernabella or Alice Springs, no worries.

Rupert Goodwin

Sweet liquid from grevillea and other sweet flowers can be sucked from the plants or mixed with water to make a cordial-like drink.

Some foods, such as these ripe bush figs found growing at the base of Uluṟu, are eaten as soon as they are picked.

Some bush foods

Diary
Friday 27th June

Mantajarra had promised to take the kids out for honey-ants if they cleaned up the yard. They'd done the job and so Mantajarra, five children and I climbed into the Toyota and drove over to the neighbour's house where we picked up Topsy. Digging sticks and *wira* (small cup-like digging scoops) are thrown in through the car windows and then we drive off towards Kata Tjuta. After nearly an hour, we turn off onto a dirt road. The sand beneath the tyres is a deep red and the ground is covered with yellow spinifex and squat mulga trees. Here and there I can see the tracks of animals. By now the kids have all fallen asleep in the afternoon warmth. Although it's the middle of winter, the temperature still rises to mid-twenties in the desert. We drive through the scrub. Topsy and Mantajarra talk constantly – they are looking for tracks and holes beneath the trees that show signs of animal activity. Eventually they decide on a spot and, beneath the shade of mulga trees, Topsy begins to loosen the earth with a crow-bar.

As the loose earth falls away Topsy removes it with her bowl, *wira*, and Mantajarra helps with a small spade. Eventually she finds a cavity and begins to move the earth extremely gently. A hole is revealed and deep inside it I can see the round shiny engorged bodies of several honey-ants. Topsy strips a small twig of bark and gently tucks it into the cavity, pulling out six or seven honey-ants. Everything is done very carefully at this stage as the ants are delicate and it would be easy to break the sac which holds the honey and lose it in the sand. Mantajarra hands me the first ant and tells me, 'try it, your first honey-ant'. She shows me how to hold onto the body with my fingers and pull off the honey sac with my tongue. As it bursts, my mouth is filled with its sweetness, like nectar from flowers. The women carry on digging all afternoon. We eat our fill and load three bowls with ants to take back for the grandchildren. Mantajarra shows me how to squeeze the bodies to kill the ants, she tells me this way they can be kept for one or two weeks. Mantajarra likes taking the kids out looking for honey-ants because she enjoys teaching them about traditional ways of life.

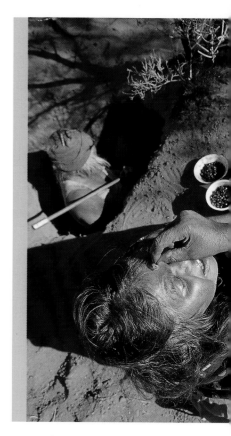

Mantajarra bursting on her forehead one of the first honey ants we find. This is the Anangu custom to show respect for the Tjukurpa pertaining to the honey ant.

Arnguli, bush plum

The bush plum is shaped like a gumnut and is found on small shrubby bushes. There are many of these bushes around the base of Uluru. They bear fruit even in the cold months of June and July. The plums begin as a green colour and gradually darken to an almost black colour. This is when Anangu know the fruit is ripe and ready to eat. Traditionally the bush plum is warmed in the coals of the fire and then the pulp is squeezed and water is added to it. The liquid, a little like a soup, is called *awalyuru*. Bush plum can also be eaten straight from the tree or dried and reconstituted later using water and heat.

As well as honey-ants, women also gather small lizards, *ngintaka*. Their yellow eggs are highly prized and, like the lizards, are cooked in the coals of the fire. According to a film presented in the Cultural Centre, pregnant women avoid eating *ngintaka* as it is said that their child may be born with scaly skin.

Another favourite bush food are *maku*, witchetty grubs. These are threaded together on twine strands and placed in the coals of the fire for a few minutes. The insides are initially runny and yellow but after cooking they set firm, a bit like an egg. Women also hunt rabbits with their digging sticks. They lick the end of the stick and push them down the rabbit holes, if the stick emerges with any fur on it, they know a rabbit may well be in the hole.

Maku, witchetty grubs

Medicine

Plant medicine

Many fruits and berries gathered by Anangu have medicinal properties and were made into drinks or pastes that were often placed on the skin or around the head as a cap to reduce fevers. Anaja is a native fuscia which is ground up with a grinding stone. Water is then added and the mixture makes a hard paste which is rubbed all over the body to ease and relieve pain. Wayunu, or quondong, is made into a paste by grinding the nut and mixing it with water. This paste is smeared onto the head or back to relieve headache or backaches. It can also be used as a hair conditioner.

Droppings of the zebra finch are crushed and mixed with water into a paste. This medicine is used to relieve sore eyes and also for burns. The droppings are usually taken from the birds' nests which are often found close to waterholes.

'Wiru ninti nyinanytja – Learning to stay well', poster produced by Nganampa Health Council in Alice Springs. This and similar posters use traditional dot style painting and symbols to describe contemporary health problems and solutions.

My grandmother showed me the bush medicine for boiling with water and drinking or making oil and putting it on the head for headache and other one for burning, all from the bush, bush medicine. Sometimes boil up margarine oil and mix with plants and use 'em like a paste. Long time ago, early-days, people in the beginning, if people get a burn in the fire they use that paste like a bandage. Before margarine, we using water, we're making new way now, different way.
Nellie Patterson

Healers

There are a number of healers living in Anangu communities. People go to them and ask them to remove the illness from a sick person. They often do this by sucking the bad blood from the sick person through a small incision.

Alukura – traditional birthing centre

Traditionally Anangu women gave birth to their children in the bush. Childbirth was very much a woman's domain and traditional midwives took charge. Men had nothing to do with the experience – childbirth is sacred law for women. The actual location or area of country in which babies were born became an extremely important and significant place for the children. The placenta is buried in the birth place as a way of linking the child, the mother and the earth. Today some women still give birth in the bush, but increasing numbers have their children in hospitals. They have been told that this is more hygienic and safer should the birth be complicated. However hospitals are also very alien and often don't allow for the grandmothers and aunties, who would have attended a traditional birth, to be present. This means many Aboriginal women feel quite alone and often scared in these environments. The presence of male doctors in many hospitals is a cause of shame to Aboriginal women. Neither do ordinary hospitals take into account some of the traditional practices still considered important by many Anangu.

In response to this the Alukura Birthing Centre has developed. Located in Alice Springs, Alukura offers Aboriginal women a safe, clean environment in which to give birth to their children, but it also respects tradition. Traditional grandmothers make up part of the hospital staff. They ensure certain traditional practices are observed. Important food taboos are taken into account. Babies have the smoke of an open fire fanned over them after the birth. This is a common Aboriginal practice believed to help babies grow healthy and strong. In hospitals the placenta is usually incinerated, which many women feel may make their children sick. At Alukura, traditional practices are followed.

People still living in bush use bush-medicine. People use man witch-doctor and woman witch-doctor. They're pretty important. Witch-doctor pulls sickness away, draws the blood away with the mouth, sucking away and taking away the rubbish. Still got some witch-doctor here, maybe woman or man. If the witch-doctor far away somewhere people might pass away.
Rupert Goodwin

'Tjukurpa Irititja Munu Kuwaritja – A story of past and present' This poster hangs on the wall in the Mutitjulu clinic.

Social relationships

Social relationships are of great significance for Anangu. Families are large and extended. If a child's mother has several sisters, these sisters all take on the role of mother to that child, particularly for ceremonial purposes. Likewise, all the father's brothers take on the role of father to his son. However, the father's sister's husband, the child's uncle, is considered a distant relation. He is not close to the child – in fact there is a certain amount of avoidance within their relationship. Avoidance relationships take place between particular relatives and mean that they will rarely have direct contact, particularly during ceremonial times. If a young girl wishes to communicate with her uncle she might send a message through another member of the family. These relationships are not strictly observed today.

Marriage

When a boy becomes a man, a number of parents will promise their daughters to him. One girl will be chosen and when she reaches a marriageable age the man she is promised to will give gifts of food and money to her parents. Traditionally he would follow the family as they travelled and a member of the girl's family, usually a brother, would eventually take her to him. When they set up camp together they were considered married. If a young girl runs away with another man before she is married, then that man will have to give gifts, not only to the girl's family, but also to the man to whom she was promised. Traditionally men often had more than one wife, perhaps two or three though this is rare today.

Death

When a death occurs Anangu experience great sorrow. Their grief is so great that the name of a dead person can not be used for a length of time, and if any other person in the community has the same name, it is either changed or they are called *kunmanara*. If any word in the vocabulary has a similar sound to that of the dead person's name, this word is also replaced by *kunmanara*. The sound of the person's name provokes feelings of grief amongst mourning relatives and for this reason it is avoided. If the person is thought to have died in the prime of their life or in tragic circumstances, the name or word may not be used for as many as 15 or 20 years. It is also forbidden to look at photographs of a dead person until the community consider a reasonable amount of time has passed since their death. In the Cultural Centre there are several photographs which have been covered with pieces of card because they show the image of a deceased person. Again, this is to avoid causing the relatives unnecessary sorrow.

Traditionally those who died were buried in large holes in the ground and covered with grass and branches. Logs were then placed across the top of the opening and a piece of gum sapling was placed in a mound of earth to one end. If the dead person were a man, this gum sapling represented his spear. If it were a woman, the sapling represented her digging stick. Anangu are now generally buried at the cemetery.

Our grandmothers are the ones who teach us about who we are connected to, how we must respect this person, the relationships that we have. They have all that knowledge. We learn as we get older about our connections to other people.
Karina Lester

Barbara Tjikatu and her grandchildren

Leo Watson, Frank Charles and
Leon Jingo at Muṯitjulu
holding one of the bowls
sold by Maraku Arts

Weapons, tools and utensils

Spear – kulata

Anangu use numerous tools, weapons and utensils. Most of these are made from combinations of plant and animal materials. All young girls and boys learn at an early age how to make the objects used for hunting and gathering food. One of the first things a young boy learns is how to make a hunting spear, or *kulata*. The spear is about three metres long and made from flexible vine. Long vine branches are heated over a small fire and made as straight as possible. The vine itself is quite light – a heavier, harder piece of wood is used to craft the spearhead. The spearhead is lashed on with kangaroo sinews and *kiti*, spinifex glue. Spears are often thrown from spearthrowers, *miru*.

Spearthrower – miru

The *miru* is used to add length to the arm throwing the spear, allowing it to be thrown further. It also has several other uses. A curved, almost bowl-like shape, the *miru* can be used as a container and as a fire-maker. One side is used to create friction against another piece of hardwood. This produces intense heat against which small clumps of dry spinifex grass are held until they ignite. Shields, *tara*, were made and often used in combat, but the *miru* also served as a shield during fighting.

Boomerangs – kali

Boomerangs, *kali*, are usually made of mulga wood and used for hunting. Sometimes they are cut with designs which relate to the owner's ceremonies or birthplace. Though they are most often used for hunting, they also double as a musical instrument. Two boomerangs can be banged together during the songs and dances which form part of ceremonies.

Clubs and chisels – tjutinypa, kantitjara

Clubs are used for many purposes: hunting, fighting and ceremony. *Tjutinypa* are used only by men. They are long and have a piece of quartz rock on one end, which has been stuck into a lump of spinifex resin that is moulded onto the wooden handle. This club is most often used for hunting. A *walayiti* is flatter and traditionally used for fighting. *Kantitjara* is a name which applies to a range of tools used by men for making and decorating their weapons. Women also use a club called a *kuturu*, mostly for self-defence.

Bowls – piti, kanilpa, wira

Piti, *kanilpa* and *wira* are commonly called coolamons but this is not a traditional name. A<u>n</u>angu usually cut bowls from white gum or mulga bark or river red gum roots. Circular shapes are cut with chisels or contemporary axes. These pieces of circular bark are carved and shaped. As they dry, the sides curl upwards forming a bowl. Small sticks are used to stop the bowls curling too far.

The *piti* is the largest bowl and is commonly used for collecting water. Women sometimes used *kiti*, spinifex glue, to block the ends of the bowl so that it could hold more liquid. *Piti* are also used to carry food and other belongings and are balanced on the head on top of a round head-ring. Traditionally these rings were made with human hair but today they are usually made of wool. The *kanilpa* is a smaller and narrower bowl and is used by women for collecting seed from spinifex grass. They hold it against spinifex grass, pulling the plant so that the small seeds fall off into the bowl. It is also used for sifting edible grass seeds. The smallest bowl, the *wira*, is used as a scoop and a digging implement, perhaps for digging honey-ants or looking for water below the ground.

A mark left in the trunk of a tree from which the bark and carnbium layer has been removed to make a bowl.

As the bowls dry, small twigs of various lengths are placed across them so the sides are forced to remain apart at the desired distance. This ranger is giving a demonstration to tourists. He is also holding a miru, spearthrower.

Arts

Maraku Arts

Maraku Arts is a commercial outlet for contemporary Anangu art. It sells numerous crafts to tourists at Uluru-Kata Tjuta and to galleries in Australia and overseas. The organisation involves 15 Aboriginal communities and buys art work from over 800 craftspeople. About once every six weeks people from Maraku Arts travel out to the communities. When they arrive they put a number of large plastic tubs in a semi-circle and artists put carvings they've made into the tubs, depending on size and price of each piece.

Management

Maraku Arts has a board which meets every three months and is made up of one representative from each of the member communities. These representatives are voted in by each community. Meetings are used to discuss business issues. Maraku Arts was originally started on a small grant from the federal government's Aboriginal Arts Board and has grown to be one of the largest Aboriginal artist-owned- and- controlled arts centres in Australia.

Many animals are carved, mostly from the root of the river red gum, but sometimes from mulga. Lots of wooden animals are sold. Some of the most popular are the goanna, ngintaka, the poisonous snake, liru, the python, kuniya, and the echidna, tjilkamata. These animals are decorated with either traditional design work or natural markings. All carvings are oiled with a mixture that is half linseed oil and half turpentine. The linseed oil prevents cracking and the turpentine kills borers and mites.

Billy Wara using the hot wire to make patterns on the carved goanna.

Keeping culture alive

People from Muṯitjulu also produce many beautiful dot paintings. The paintings are based on traditional sand paintings – designs drawn in the sand often for ceremony and later erased. The paintings usually tell stories, from the Tjukurpa. Sometimes they are produced by small children who have been taught the stories by their parents. Maraku artists do produce some entirely contemporary work, however most of the crafts for sale draw from traditional culture. Maraku Arts is an important part of keeping Aboriginal culture alive and at the same time it provides Aṉangu with an income.

I been teaching like cutting trees for making toys animal and small little spear. Sometimes we go out for creek and I cut river gum root and teach them when I'm cutting. I make little bird, big bird, goanna and teach 'em everything. Important culture, culture one, education, teaching whitefella way, teaching traditional way. I teaching proper way. The whitefella teaching white way, this is traditional owners, teaching traditional owner way.

Nellie Patterson

Diary
Monday 30th July
Sitting by the fire in his yard, Billy Wara has six or seven thick pieces of wire lying in the white-hot ashes of the fire. He is working with a carved wooden goanna which is just over a metre long. He takes out one of the wires and rubs it gently across the back of the goanna, turning the timber a dark brown-black colour as it burns. Billy works around the numerous circular marks already scalded onto the creature's back. As each piece of wire cools, he returns it to the fire, drawing out another and continuing with the work. To create the circular shapes he presses crescent-shaped pieces of wire into the wood, then rotates the carving and repeats the action from the other side. He sits, as the sun drops, until the whole goanna has been covered with the design. Tomorrow he will take it to Maraku Arts to be sold in the shop at the Cultural Centre.

Tourism

In 1948 a dirt road was made and Uluru became accessible to tourists. As the park became an increasingly popular destination, the natural environment and Anangu sacred sites were damaged. In an effort to relieve the impact of tourists and support the tourist industry, Yulara Resort was built. Until 1984, tourists had stayed in motels and caravan parks close to Uluru and the Mutitjulu community, but now they stay at Yulara which is outside the national park. Figures on display at the Cultural Centre show that in 1987, 216 000 people visited the park. In 1997, the park had 350 000 visitors.

Anangu Tours

Anangu Tours is a tour company owned by Anangu people. It runs a number of tours, all of which concentrate on teaching tourists about traditional Anangu culture and ways of seeing the land. All tours are conducted by one or two Anangu and an interpreter, often themselves Anangu. On one of the tours, tourists learn about the Mutitjulu waterhole and its importance to Anangu. They are introduced to a number of local bush foods and taught something of the *Kuniya* Tjukurpa, woma python snake dreaming. The *Kuniya* Tjukurpa can be seen in the rock itself. The Anangu tour leaders point out a winding band of rock stretching across the surface of Uluru. They explain that this is *Kuniya* moving in to attack *Liru*, the poisonous snake, as told in the Tjukurpa.

Anangu and non-Anangu park staff worked together to determine which were the most culturally and environmentally appropriate sunset and sunrise viewing areas for the large numbers of tourists who visit the park.

PARK IN MARKED AREA

Diary

Wednesday 2nd July

There were about 30 people on the tour including several children. As we walked along the liru track heading towards Ulu_ru we came upon a small shelter or *wurli* where a fire was already burning and large logs were positioned as seats. Tiku, one of the A_nangu guides, began to beat a handful of spinifex, a special resinous grass. As the leaves quickly fell from the plant a fine residue of powder appeared on the ground. Tiku then gathered up the leaves and placed them in the fire, she moved the branches and gently scraped up the powder into a small bowl which was passed around for everyone to see. After this she took a stick from her bag on either end of which were large circular blobs of spinifex glue or *kiti*. Tiku heated these balls over the fire until they became sticky and rolled them across the dry powder. The powder stuck to the surface and when Tiku held it across the flames, it quickly melted to form the brown resin-like substance which is *kiti*. At the same time Tiku spat on her fingers and used the moisture to cool and shape the glue until the ball was again smooth and shiny.

Making balls of kiti, spinifex glue.

Karina Lester, one of the interpreters working with A_nangu Tours, watches as tourists attempt to throw the kulata (spear) with the miru (spearthrower) during one of the company's tours.

When designing something such as a shade structure, Aboriginal people know what tourists are going to do because they've been watching them for decades. They know where they are going to sit down, where they are going to want to photograph, where the shade will be at all different times of the day, how that is going to change during the year, what the impact of dust is going to be.

Julian Barry, former training officer and park manager

Cultural Centre

My job here is to answer to all sorts of questions the tourists ask – give them information about everything and anything: How do you find water? How did old people make fire? How did the rock come to be? I answer letters from students, people all over the world – some ring, some fax. They want information about the park, how we run it, look after it. The Cultural Centre is an important place because it's got all the Tjukurpa. You go to church – they got all the script there, stuff that's important to them. Well this is the same for Anangu people. This is a strong place for education and religion.

Les Calma, one of the Anangu park staff who looks after the learning area at the Cultural Centre

Insensitivity

When tourists first began to visit Uluru and Kata Tjuta they had little understanding of Anangu culture. As a result, visitors wandered into sacred sites, some of which Anangu women and children are not allowed to access. People began to climb Uluru which was deeply upsetting to the traditional landowners because the path cut across the tracks of the *mala*, hare wallaby. In an effort to teach tourists more about Anangu culture, a Cultural Centre was set up. There people can learn through a combination of stories, pictures, audio visual displays and sound panels.

Cultural Centre

The 10th anniversary of the handback of the park to its Traditional Owners was celebrated with the opening of the Cultural Centre in 1995. The Cultural Centre embodies the principle of 'working together' in its conception, design and content. The architect worked closely with the Anangu and lived in the community for some time, establishing relationships and trust with the people prior to working on the design. Anangu pointed out to the architect that they wanted visitors to understand that Uluru was filled with stories from the Tjukurpa and that its natural formations reflected these stories. They wanted tourists to understand that whenever they look at certain parts of the rock, they are reminded of the creation journeys – Uluru is like a book of stories.

The Cultural Centre is made, as far as possible, from local materials. It is built from mud bricks made from local earth. The beams, supports and lintels are made of plantation-grown native cypress and yellow box. The roof tiles are made of copper and wooden shingles, and are designed to look like the scales of a snake. There is an oval-shaped opening, like the eye of the snake in the roof between an area called the Tjukurpa tunnel and the learning area. The Cultural Centre provides a wonderful place for visitors to learn more about Anangu way of life – to begin to understand Uluru–Kata Tjuta National Park through Anangu eyes.

The Cultural Centre was designed to reflect certain aspects of the Tjukurpa stories which relate to Liru (poisonous snake) and Kuniya (python). The shapes of these creatures are echoed in the shape and form of many aspects of the building. In the learning centre, small circular areas provide information on Anangu culture and customs. These circular shapes relate to the shape of the Kuniya's eggs.

In the Cultural Centre there is a touch wall on which a variety of Tjukurpa symbols are depicted in bas-relief by artists, Barbara Tjikatu and Rene Kulijta. The wall is designed for blind people so they can feel the objects and get an idea of their shape and form. A small panel of braille provides information about the objects.

One senior traditional owner said: 'That tourist comes here with a camera taking pictures all over. What has he got? Another photo – take home keep part of Uluru. He should get another lens – see straight inside. He wouldn't see that big rock then. He would see that *kuniya* living right inside there as from the beginning. He might throw his camera away then.'
Tony Tjamiwa, teaching about Anangu culture at Uluru–Kata Tjuta National Park, from the Park Notes

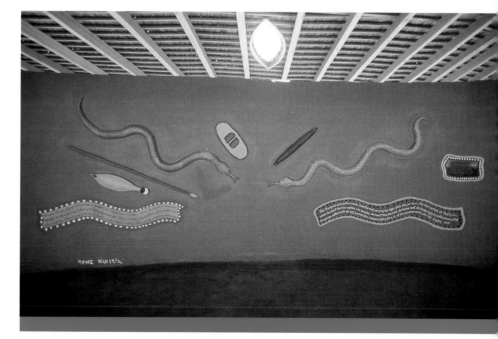

The Tjukurpa tunnel

The Cultural Centre design was based on the Tjukurpa stories of the *Liru*, poisonous snake, and the *Kuniya*, python. As you walk around the exterior mud brick walls you hear the sound of animals and birds from Uluru, and Anangu singing. You then enter through the Tjukurpa tunnel which represents the inside of the stomach of the *kuniya*. In this area, Tjukurpa stories are written on the walls along with descriptions and pictures of the kinds of food Anangu women gathered. Grinding stones, digging sticks and bowls are displayed. Beautiful tiles, also made by Anangu, are painted with *maku* (witchetty grubs), goanna, bush foods, fruits and medicines. On the opposite side of the tunnel is the men's area, displaying spears, spearthrowers and tiles painted with boomerangs, animal tracks and weapons for hunting. The walls of the tunnel wind and bend like the movement of a snake. Even the bench seats are shaped like snakes.

This floor mosaic was designed by Barbara Tjikatu to tell her story about teaching the 'whitefella' about Tjukurpa.

Relatives of some of those who died climbing Uluru have placed memorial plaques on the side of the rock.

Anangu nganana tatintja wiya

At the end of the tunnel is a sign which reads *Anangu nganana tatintja wiya*. It translates as *Anangu never climb Uluru*. The sign explains that Anangu hope that by the time visitors have travelled through the tunnel they will understand why the Aboriginal owners prefer them not to climb the rock. The notice explains Uluru is the Anangu's home, it is a place of food, gathering and waterholes. It is also an Anangu place of knowledge and learning about the Tjukurpa. It is a sacred and religious place – the path taken by visitors is also the path taken by the *mala* men in preparation for their ceremonies. When visitors die on the rock, Anangu people feel personally responsible and grieve for the dead. For all these reasons Anangu prefer that visitors don't climb.

Tjukurpa, meeting for black fella and white fella, that's why. Make footprint for black skin and shoes, like you gottim shoes, that's for whitefella. They sit down, talking for meeting, learning my language. Blackfella learning English sharing that like language, talking for language, talking honey-ants, bush tucker, goanna, kangeroo, learning for Tjukurpa. That's why we learning them, some whitefella come, no reading, no learning, he want to climb, he maybe fall down, he don't know that probably someone fall down. Sorry everybody, everybody sorry. That's why we writing, we tell 'em that Tjukurpa, don't climb, something might happen.
Barbara Tjikatu

Conclusion

Change

Many things have changed in the lives of the A<u>n</u>angu. They now live more settled lives. Young children go to school and learn to speak English. Many new foods have meant that hunting and gathering is not a necessity, and instead money is required in order to shop at the store. The desire for new material goods, like guns, cars, clothes, and fuel, means that A<u>n</u>angu have had to find ways of earning money. The church has brought new spiritual ideas to the community. Western medicine has introduced new ways of healing and alternatives to traditional herbs and healers. Television, radio, tourists, white rangers and community advisors have all entered the community introducing new ideas, attitudes and experiences. The loss of land and the ensuing struggle to achieve handback and joint management of Uluru–Kata Tju<u>t</u>a have involved A<u>n</u>angu in politics and non-Aboriginal law. They have regained a certain amount of control over land where they are the Traditional Owners.

Judy Trigger taking part in Kuniya women's inma, the ceremony of the woma python

Problems

One of the greatest problems that has arisen as a result of many of the changes is the lack of direction for the younger people. Whilst young teenagers would traditionally have been occupied by the necessity of finding food, by the conducting of ceremony and the learning of traditional law, these things have changed. Whilst they are still taught of the Tjukurpa and this knowledge remains strong, there is no longer a need to hunt and gather and ceremony is not conducted as frequently as it was in the past. Young people finish school in their early teens. Most have no desire to travel away from their community to find work and many adolescents lose their sense of direction. Alcohol abuse and petrol sniffing amongst the young have become serious problems not only for Mu<u>t</u>itjulu but for many other Aboriginal communities.

Collaboration

Since the handback of Uluru–Kata Tjuta to its Traditional Owners, Anangu have begun to regain control over their own lives and over the way in which their land is managed. This has led to successful joint management of the running of the Uluru–Kata Tjuta National Park, which has resulted in a very effective sharing of traditional Anangu knowledge and non-Aboriginal knowledge. The information which results from this collaboration is used to protect both the cultural and environmental aspects of the park and the people who visit it. The fauna survey and the introduction of land management through patch burning illustrate how effective 'working together' can be. The Board of Management ensures that Anangu continue to have a great deal of control over the ways in which their country is managed and that they are able to discuss new issues to determine the best approach for the community's interests and for the park itself.

Organisations like Maraku Arts, which draws on tradition to produce commercially saleable contemporary art, help to create appropriate employment for all ages. Anangu Tours provides employment based on teaching tourists about traditional ways of life.

Tjukurpa today

The joint management of Uluru–Kata Tjuta National Park ensures that Tjukurpa stories are respected and sacred sites are maintained. Through various arrangements established by Anangu, tourists are taught about the Tjukurpa in the hope that a better understanding will help them develop a richer appreciation and understanding of the cultural value and importance of Uluru–Kata Tjuta.

Looking towards Kata Tjuta

Contemporary art incorporates aspects of traditional design and provides a source of income for artists at Mutitjulu. This bowl was made by Jennifer Taylor.

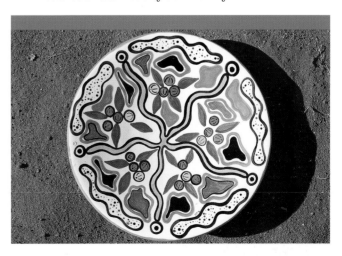

Desert flower

Glossary

Aboriginal Land Rights Act a federal law passed in 1976 which enabled Aboriginal people to claim ownership of unalienated land

arnguli bush plum

assimilation absorbing one culture into another so that it, in effect, disappears

bush tucker foods such as berries, seeds, honey-ants and witchetty grubs, found in the bush

handback ceremony in 1985 when Uluru–Kata Tjuta National Park was officially handed back to its Traditional Owners

initiation a ceremony conducted for Aboriginal boys and girls whereby they become men and women

kali throwing stick or boomerang

kanilpa shallow wooden bowl used by women for collecting seeds

kiti spinifex glue

kulata wooden hunting spear

kuniya woma python

kunmanara word used in place of the name of a person who has recently died, and in place of any words that sound like the person's name

kuturu women's fighting club

liru poisonous snake

lungkata blue-tongued lizard

maku witchetty grub

mala Rufous hare wallaby

miru spearthower or woomera

mission settlement set up by Christian missionaries to convert Aboriginal people to Christianity

ngintaka very large monitor lizard

nomadic people who don't live in one settled place but move across the land looking for food and water

pastoralists graziers who run cattle or sheep

patch burning deliberately setting fire to parts of the bush to help with land management

piti a large bowl used for carrying water or food and other belongings

reserves areas of land set aside in the 1930s for exclusive use by Aboriginal people

sacred sites places in the landscape that have spiritual significance to the indigenous people

sovereign supreme ruler

subsistence existence living off the land so that everything that is needed for survival is taken directly from the environment

tara wooden shield

terra nullius a term meaning empty land, used by Europeans when they first arrived in Australia as a legal reason to declare that the land was not owned by the indigenous inhabitants

Tjukurpa a body of knowledge that contains information about Aboriginal law and religious beliefs; also spelt *Tjukurrpa* by some Aboriginal groups

tjutinypa club with a quartz head

Traditional Owners Aboriginal people with primary responsibility for looking after a particular area of land

unalienated crown land crown land, over which no one holds a mining, pastoral or commercial lease

walayiti a hunting club

wayunu quondong, a kind of shrub or small tree with bright red fruit

wiltja a shelter built of tree branches and spinifex to protect from wind and rain

wira a bowl used as a scoop or digging tool

woomera spearthrower

working together a system adopted at Uluru whereby Anangu and non-Anangu people are jointly involved in the management of the park

Further reading

An Insight into Uluru: the Mala Walk and the Mutitjulu Walk, Uluru–Kata Tjuta National Park

Breeden, S. *Growing up at Uluru Australia*, Steve Parish Publishing, QLD, 1995

Breeden, S. *Uluru: Looking After Uluru–Kata Tjuta – The Anangu Way*, Simon and Schuster, Sydney, 1994

Goddard, C. (ed) *Pitjantjatjara/Yankuntjatjara to English Dictionary*, 2nd edition, IAD Press, 1996

Institute for Aboriginal Development, *Sharing the Park – Anangu initiatives in Ayers Rock Tourism*, Asprint, Alice Springs, 1987

Isaacs, J. *Desert Crafts, Anangu Maruku Punu*, Doubleday, Sydney, 1992

Layton, R. *Uluru – An Aboriginal History of Ayers Rock*, Australian Institute of Aboriginal Studies, Canberra, 1986

Mutitjulu Community, *Mingkiri, a natural history of Uluru*, IAD Press, 1996

Index